Here's to Sue!

By Lindsay Carlson

To Sue, the best mom and most devoted teacher. Each student you had was lucky to be in your class. Hope this captures some memories from your journey. Happy Retirement!

Love,

Lindsay

Find the hidden apple on each page!

In San Mateo, where dreams take flight, lived a girl named Sue, with a future bright.

From her earliest days, she held a clear view; teaching little ones was what she wanted to do.

Off to Sac State, Sue eagerly went, with dreams of teaching, her heart content.

She soaked up the knowledge, each lesson a treasure, her heart set on teaching, a lifelong pleasure.

With diploma gleaming, she took the stand, a teacher born, with book in hand.

Her classroom filled with laughter and cheer, as she taught her students year after year.

	1	2	3	4	5	6	7	8	9	10
1	1	2	3	4	5	6	7	8	9	10
2	2	4	6	8	10	12	14	16	18	20
3	3	6	9	12	15	18	21	24	27	30
4	4	8	12	16	20	24	28	32	36	40
5	5	10	15	20	25	30	35	40	45	50
6	6	12	18	24	30	36	42	48	54	60
7	7	14	21	28	35	42	49	56	63	70
8	8	16	24	32	40	48	56	64	72	80
9	9	18	27	36	45	54	63	72	81	90
10	10	20	30	40	50	60	70	80	90	100

Then came John, her love and partner true, together they built a family, first one daughter, then two.

Balancing home and school with grace, Sue found happiness in each place. She taught with love, day after day, watching her students and daughters learn and play.

For four decades she shared her light, guiding young minds, from morning till night.

But as time whispered gently, its soft, sweet refrain, retirement beckoned, a new chapter to gain.

Sue had joyful tears in her eyes as the day finally came for her sweet goodbyes.

With fond farewells, she closed the door,

on teaching days, forevermore.

So here's to Sue! A teacher, a wife, a mother so dear, her legacy of love will always be near.

CONGRATULATIONS

Her story's not over, the
next chapter has just begun,
retirement adventures await,
filled with laughter and fun!

www.ingramcontent.com/pod-product-compliance
Ingram Content Group UK Ltd.
Pitfield, Milton Keynes, MK11 3LW, UK
UKHW061940050826
14089UKWH00045BA/178